THINK AND ACT LIKE A MILLIONAIRE

THE PATH TO MILLIONAIRE
MINDSET ESSENTIALS STRATEGIES FOR FINANCIAL SUCCESS

BY

JOHNSON RYAN

TABLE OF CONTENTS

INTRODUCTION

The process of cultivating and adopting the mindset or style of thinking necessary to achieve financial success and become a Millionaire is referred to as "The Path to Millionaire Mindset." It suggests a sequence of actions, shifts in viewpoint, and maybe specific routines or habits that people might adopt in order to develop the kind of thinking linked to prosperous wealth development.

The idea that everything is achievable with effort and commitment is part of the "Path to Millionaire" worldview. The Millionaire Mindset Path teaches us that achieving financial objectives requires time, effort, dedication, and sacrifice rather than just luck. They also think that planning ahead and taking measured chances when they arise are important.

In essence, it proposes a metamorphic procedure meant to bring one's beliefs and dispositions into harmony with the values and tactics that millionaires frequently credit for their achievements.

As a basic section of the book, "The Path to Millionaire Mindset" introduces the reader to the concepts and ideas that will be covered in later sections. Here's a more thorough explanation:

1. **Understanding the Millionaire Mindset:**Introduce the concept of a "millionaire mindset," explaining that it goes beyond financial aspects and encompasses a set of attitudes, beliefs, and approaches that successful individuals share.

2. **Shifting your Mindset:**Discuss why mindset is a crucial factor in achieving financial success. Emphasize how one's thoughts and attitudes toward money can significantly impact their actions and decisions.

3. **Myths and Realities:**Address common misconceptions about wealth creation and debunk myths that might hinder readers from developing a positive and effective mindset for financial success.

4. **Personal Stories or Examples**:Share real-life examples or anecdotes of individuals who transformed their mindset and achieved financial prosperity. This can provide inspiration and tangible evidence of the power of mindset shifts.

5. **Reader's Self-Reflection**:Encourage readers to reflect on their current mindset and attitudes towards money. Pose questions or prompts that prompt self-awareness and introspection.

6. **Purpose of the Book**:Clearly outline the purpose and goals of the book. Explain how it aims to guide readers through practical strategies and insights to develop a millionaire mindset and ultimately achieve financial goals.

7. **Roadmap for the Book**:Provide a brief overview of the chapters or key sections that will follow, giving readers a roadmap for what they can expect in the upcoming pages.

In essence, the introduction sets the stage for the reader's journey toward adopting a mindset conducive to financial success, fostering a sense of anticipation and understanding about the transformative process they are about to embark upon.

Understanding the Millionaire Mindset

Understanding the millionaire mindset involves delving into Essentials strategies for Financial Success. Here's an exploration of this concept:

Financial Vision: Millionaires often have a clear vision of their financial goals. Understanding the millionaire mindset involves crafting a vision for one's financial future, setting specific and achievable goals.

Risk-Taking and Investment: The millionaire mindset embraces calculated risk-taking and strategic investments. It involves recognizing opportunities, assessing risks, and making informed investment decisions to grow wealth over time.

Continuous Learning: Adopting a millionaire mindset entails a commitment to lifelong learning. Successful individuals constantly seek knowledge about financial markets, trends, and innovative wealth-building strategies.

Resilience and Persistence: Understanding the millionaire mindset requires acknowledging the importance of resilience and persistence in the face of challenges. Millionaires often encounter setbacks but maintain a determined attitude toward their financial objectives.

Focus on Value Creation: The millionaire mindset emphasizes creating value. Whether through entrepreneurship or strategic career choices, individuals with this mindset focus on contributing value to others, which often translates into financial success.

Adaptability to Change: Embracing change and adapting to evolving economic landscapes are key aspects of the millionaire mindset. This involves staying flexible, adjusting strategies as needed, and being open to new opportunities.

Financial Discipline:Millionaires exhibit disciplined financial habits. This includes budgeting, saving consistently, and avoiding unnecessary debt. Understanding the mindset involves adopting these disciplined financial practices.

Mindfulness and Gratitude:Cultivating mindfulness and gratitude is integral to the millionaire mindset. Appreciating one's current financial state and being mindful of spending habits contribute to a positive and abundant mindset.

To Put It Simply, understanding the millionaire mindset goes beyond surface-level perceptions of wealth. It involves adopting a set of attitudes, behaviors, and strategies that align with the principles practiced by those who have successfully created and maintained substantial wealth. By incorporating these Essentials strategies, individuals can work towards achieving financial Success and developing their own millionaire mindset.

CHAPTER 1: SHIFTING YOUR MINDSET

DEFINITION

The purposeful and conscious effort to change your attitudes, convictions, and points of view toward a particular area of your life is known as "shifting your mindset"; this is often done in order to overcome challenges or make personal growth. Rethinking money, achievement, and financial possibilities are all components of shifting your viewpoint on developing wealth or personal finance.

It also means shifting from a worldview of scarcity—that is, thinking there isn't enough for everyone—to one of abundance—that is, thinking there are plenty of opportunities to succeed. It could also mean facing and changing self-limiting beliefs about your ability to make money, take sensible risks, or achieve financial goals.Changing your viewpoint is a proactive first step toward developing a more positive, empowered, and solution-focused outlook.

Shifting Your Mindset: The Key to Financial Transformation

A key idea in the path described in "Think and Act Like a Millionaire: The Path to Millionaire Mindset" is changing your perspective. This life-changing approach isn't just about getting rich; it's also about radically changing the way you think about and handle money, opportunity, and success.

Recognizing the Need for Change: Recognizing limiting beliefs and mental patterns that could impede financial progress is the first step towards understanding the need for change. Doubts about one's capacity to amass riches, a fear of taking calculated risks, or a scarcity mentality—the idea that resources are limited—are examples of these restricting beliefs.

Embracing abundant: Adopting an abundant attitude is necessary to change your perspective and think like a billionaire. This entails realizing that everyone has plenty, achievement is achievable, and chances abound. It entails changing one's perspective from one of scarcity to one of abundance and cultivating an optimistic attitude that draws opportunities and riches.

Overcoming Limiting Beliefs: As obstacles to financial success, challenge and destroy limiting beliefs. Whether it's self-doubt or fear of failing, actively work on replacing these constricting ideas with empowering beliefs and affirmations that can help you on your path to becoming a Millionaire.

Adopting a Growth Mindset: A growth mindset is crucial in the pursuit of financial abundance. Instead of viewing challenges as insurmountable obstacles, see them as opportunities for learning and growth. This mindset shift encourages resilience, adaptability, and a willingness to continuously improve—qualities that are often characteristic of those who have achieved financial success.

Aligning Actions With Aspirations: Shifting your mindset is not only about changing thoughts but also about aligning actions with your financial aspirations. This may involve making strategic investments, seeking new opportunities, and embracing a proactive approach to wealth creation. It's about transforming thoughts into tangible, goal-oriented actions.

Cultivating Positive Financial Habits: As your mindset evolves, cultivate positive financial habits. This includes disciplined budgeting, consistent saving, and informed investment decisions. These habits, rooted in the millionaire mindset, become the building blocks of sustained financial success.

Constant Self-Reflection: Changing your perspective is a journey that never ends. Consider your beliefs, behaviors, and attitudes toward money on a regular basis. As you come across new chances and problems, make necessary adjustments to your mentality to keep it in line with your financial objectives.

"Think and Act Like a Millionaire" and "Shifting Your Mindset" together constitute a profound and dynamic exercise. It's about creating the mindset and habits that lead to a millionaire's path, accepting abundance, and rewriting the story of your financial life. As you go out on this path, keep in mind that the change starts in your head and manifests itself in the abundance of your material existence.

IMPORTANCE OF UNDERSTANDING SHIFTING MINDSET FOR SUCCESS

According to "Think and Act Like a Millionaire: The Path to Millionaire Mindset," mastering the concept of mental adjustment is essential to succeeding in a variety of spheres of life. Here's a look at why this change is so important:

Overcoming Limiting Beliefs: Identifying and destroying limiting beliefs that may be impeding your achievement can be done by changing your perspective. By identifying and dispelling these myths, you make room for development and success by empowering yourself and fostering a positive mindset.

Potential Untapped: Your unrealized potential can be unlocked with a changed mentality. It pushes you to venture outside your comfort zone, consider all of your options, and take measured chances. The key to succeeding in both your personal and financial efforts is this potential unleashing.

Building a Positive Feedback Loop: Good deeds and thoughts lead to good results. When you realize how important it is to change your perspective, a positive feedback loop is started. When you observe how your altered viewpoints affect your behavior and outcomes, it bolsters your confidence that success is possible and inspires you to work even harder.

Developing an Abundance Mentality: People who have an abundance mentality tend to be successful in life. Changing your perspective from one of scarcity to abundance makes you more open to chances, promotes teamwork, and supports a giving and positive outlook on life—all of which are factors in success as a whole.

Improving Adaptability and Resilience: A straight path to success is uncommon. Realizing the significance of mental changes gives you the fortitude to overcome obstacles and the flexibility to deal with shifting conditions. Maintaining this mental flexibility is essential to achieving long-term success.

Aligning Goals with Actions:Success is not just about setting goals; it's about aligning your daily actions with those goals. Shifting your mindset ensures that your thoughts and behaviors are in harmony with your aspirations. This alignment accelerates progress and increases the likelihood of achieving your desired outcomes.

Cultivating a Growth Mindset: The millionaire mindset thrives on a growth-oriented outlook. Understanding the need for a mindset shift involves embracing challenges as opportunities for learning and growth. This mindset not only accelerates personal development but also enhances your ability to adapt and innovate in pursuit of success.

Fostering a Positive Lifestyle: Success is not solely measured by financial achievements; it also encompasses a positive and fulfilling lifestyle. Shifting your mindset contributes to a more optimistic, grateful, and purpose-driven life, enhancing overall well-being and satisfaction.

To put it Simply, understanding the importance of shifting mindset for success, outlined in this book," is a transformative journey. It goes beyond financial gains, influencing every facet of your life. By recognizing the power of mindset shifts, you lay the foundation for sustained success, personal fulfillment, and a life aligned with your aspirations.

Breaking Limiting Beliefs

Breaking Limiting Beliefs: A Crucial Step in Millionaire Mindset Development

Breaking limiting ideas is a fundamental idea in "Think and Act Like a Millionaire, " An examination of this vital stage and its importance is provided below:

Finding Limiting Beliefs: The first step in the process is to identify and acknowledge the beliefs that limit your potential. Limiting beliefs are frequently deeply rooted ideas that cast doubt on one's potential to succeed financially as well as one's sense of confidence and self-worth.

Realizing Their Impact: Strict beliefs place limitations on oneself that impede one's ability to flourish financially and personally. Thoughts such as "I'm not good with money" or "Success is only for others" can be a manifestation of them. Recognizing how these attitudes are impeding your path to financial success requires that you understand their effects.

Challenging Negative Self-Talk: One of the first steps in dismantling limiting beliefs is to confront negative self-talk and transform it into affirmations of hope. Through this process, your internal dialogue changes from one of self-doubt to one of self-empowerment, creating the foundation for a mindset that is more goal-oriented and upbeat.

Examining the Source: Examine the sources of these restrictive ideas. They could be the result of prior failures, social conditioning, or experiences from childhood. It is easier to dismantle these ideas and gain insight into their irrationality when one knows where they came from.

Redefining Self-Identity: Your self-perception is frequently shaped by limiting ideas. Redefining who you are is necessary to break them. Think about your potential, strengths, and ability to evolve rather than defining yourself by your previous transgressions or perceived weaknesses.

Affirmations and visualization: These two strategies are essential for shattering limiting beliefs. Visualize yourself as the prosperous person you want to be, and tell yourself on a regular basis that you are capable of achieving financial success. By rewiring your subconscious mind, these techniques cultivate an attitude that is more empowered.

Seeking Mentorship and Support: Be in the company of positive and inspiring people. Seek guidance from those who have succeeded financially and overcome comparable limiting beliefs. Gaining knowledge and inspiration from their experiences and advice can be quite beneficial.

Taking Baby Steps: It takes time to break beyond limiting assumptions. Move a little bit outside of your comfort zone. Every accomplishment, no matter how tiny, helps you gain confidence and break through any self-limiting ideas that might have prevented you from moving on.

Developing a Growth mentality: Adopt a growth mentality that sees obstacles as chances for development and learning. When you accept that skills can be acquired with commitment and effort, you change your perspective from one that is fixed to one that embraces success and ongoing development.

Breaking through limiting ideas is essentially one of the key strategies described in "Think and Act Like a Millionaire: The Path to Millionaire Mindset." It is a life-changing process that enables people to break free from self-imposed constraints and cultivates the attitude required to achieve financial success and fulfill one's potential.

Cultivating a Positive Money Mindset

One of the most important core principles of "Think and Act Like a Millionaire:" is developing a positive money mindset. Here is a detailed examination of the significance of this technique and how it affects financial success:

Realizing the Power of ideas: Acknowledging the profound impact that ideas have on behaviors and results is the first step towards achieving financial success. A good money mindset acknowledges the influence of attitudes on financial results and actions.

Transitioning from Scarcity to Abundance: A wealth-oriented attitude surpasses the concept of scarcity. It adopts an abundant viewpoint, recognizing opportunities and paths to financial prosperity rather than focusing on perceived shortage. This change creates the conditions for drawing abundance and wealth.

Gratitude for Current Financial condition: Regardless of how things are going right now, you should be grateful for your current financial condition as part of developing a good money mindset. Acknowledging and valuing your possessions leads to a happier life and creates opportunities for additional financial success.

Affirmations and Visualization: It's important to include constructive affirmations and visualization methods in everyday routines. Consistently expressing financial prosperity and envisioning triumph embeds these constructive ideas into the unconscious mind, strengthening the conviction in accomplishing financial objectives.

Accepting Financial Education: A good outlook on money is accompanied by a desire to learn about money matters. Making a conscious effort to learn about budgeting methods, wealth-building concepts, and investing strategies enables people to make wise financial decisions.

Learning from Setbacks: A positive money attitude is characterized by optimism in the face of setbacks. People who adopt this perspective see mistakes as chances for learning and development rather than as irreversible roadblocks. Every obstacle you face turns into a step closer to your ultimate financial success.

Avoiding Comparisons: Comparisons frequently result in negativity and unhappiness. A positive money mindset is one that prioritizes individual financial objectives over continual comparisons to those of others. This promotes advancement at one's own speed and a positive relationship with money.

Philanthropy & Generosity: Giving to charities or helping others in need are examples of acts of generosity that are essential to having a healthy money perspective. Positivity toward money is strengthened by realizing how financial prosperity affects one's own well-being as well as the well-being of others.

Aligning Financial Objectives with Personal Values: Having a healthy money mentality entails matching financial objectives with values. By preventing the chase of riches from becoming divorced from one's fundamental values, this promotes a sense of fulfillment and purpose throughout one's financial path.

Honoring Financial Milestones: It's important to acknowledge and celebrate even the smallest financial successes. Recognizing accomplishments, Accepting the notion that progress is being made, and inspiring confidence in the pursuit of more ambitious financial objectives are all components of developing a positive money mentality.

As stated in "Think and Act Like a Millionaire: The Path to Millionaire Mindset Essentials Strategies for Financial Success," developing a positive money mindset is essential to attaining long-term financial success. It influences daily choices and behaviors in addition to money gains, ultimately forming a rich and satisfying financial existence.

CHAPTER 2: FINANCIAL GOALS AND PLANNING

DEFINITION

Financial goals and planning form Individuals to utilize a strategic framework consisting of financial goals and preparation to get their intended economic outcomes. This entails establishing clear goals, coming up with a plan to achieve them, and making wise choices to protect one's financial future.

In "Think and Act Like a Millionaire: The Path to Millionaire Mindset, the importance of planning and setting financial objectives comes to the fore. Here's a detailed look at how this book views planning and financial objectives as crucial steps toward developing a Millionaire mindset:

Goal Clarity: The book stresses the significance of establishing precise and well-defined financial objectives. Whether the goal is to finance education, save for a dream home, or secure a happy retirement, the first step in any financial endeavor is to establish goals that align with personal ambitions.

Goal-Setting Tip: "Think and Act Like a Millionaire" acknowledges the importance of time segmentation. It assists people in classifying their goals into short-, mid-, and long-term targets,allowing for tailored planning strategies aligned with different time horizons

Emergency Fund as a Foundation:The book underscores the role of an emergency fund as a foundational element in financial planning. Creating a financial safety net ensures individuals are equipped to handle unforeseen expenses without derailing progress toward their broader financial goals.

Financial Success through Strategic Budgeting: Budgeting is promoted as a strategic instrument for financial success. People may prioritize savings, allocate resources effectively, and make deliberate spending decisions that support their objectives for a millionaire mindset by keeping a close eye on their income and costs.

Debt Management Techniques: One of the main priorities is to address and manage debt. The book offers doable tactics for managing different kinds of debt, stressing the significance of a well-organized strategy to gradually pay off debt and reroute funds into wealth-building projects.

Investment Wisdom for money Building: The book explores investment techniques that are crucial for accumulating money. It promotes a proactive approach to wealth creation by educating readers about various investment vehicles, risk factors, and the significance of matching investment decisions with personal financial goals.

Holistic Retirement Planning: It is said that retirement planning is an all-encompassing process. In order to guarantee a financially secure post-career existence, "Think and Act Like a Millionaire" walks people through the process of establishing reasonable retirement objectives, selecting suitable retirement funds, and making consistent contributions.

Insurance as a Protective Shield: Protection against unforeseen financial losses is emphasized by the significance of insurance coverage. A person's financial security and well-being are safeguarded by insurance, as the book emphasizes with regard to health insurance and life insurance.

Continuous Review and Adaptation: The concept of constant evaluation and modification is ingrained in financial planning by the book. It urges readers to evaluate and modify their financial strategies on a regular basis in order to stay on track toward their millionaire mindset objectives, acknowledging that life circumstances and the economy change.

To sum up, "Think and Act Like a Millionaire" considers planning and financial objectives to be essential elements of developing a Millionaire mindset. The book equips readers to manage their finances with intention, purpose, and a clear plan of action by offering helpful tactics and insights.

Setting Clear Financial Goals

The Significance of Setting Clear Financial Goals in "Think and Act Like a Millionaire: The Path to Millionaire Mindset"

One of the main ideas in the book "Think and Act Like a Millionaire, is setting specific financial goals. Here's a look at why, in the context of the book, this practice is so important:

1. **Guiding Purposeful Actions:** Having specific financial objectives gives people a sense of direction and purpose. They act as guiding beacons. Through the process of setting clear goals, the book's audience is enabled to make conscious financial decisions by coordinating their activities with their larger financial goals.

2. **Making a Success Roadmap**: The book acknowledges that reaching financial success might be difficult without a plan. Well-defined financial objectives serve as checkpoints

on this journey, enabling people to divide their journey into doable segments. This methodical technique increases the probability of achieving advancement.

3. **Motivating and Inspiring Action:**The act of setting clear financial goals is inherently motivational. It ignites a sense of purpose and inspires individuals to take action. The book encourages readers to envision their desired financial future, cultivating the motivation needed to overcome obstacles and stay committed to their goals.

4. **Establishing a Metric for Progress:** Explicit financial objectives provide an objective way to gauge progress. People are able to monitor their progress toward every objective, acknowledging accomplishments and pinpointing areas that could need modification. The millionaire mindset is strengthened and encouraged by this quantifiable progress.

5. **Establishing Clearly Defined Financial objectives:** Establishing clearly defined financial objectives fosters focus and discipline. It necessitates that people rank their goals and distribute resources appropriately. This methodical approach is essential to developing the kind of thinking required for long-term financial success.

6. **Promoting Strategic Decision-Making:** The book places a strong emphasis on the idea that strategic decision-making is guided by specific financial objectives. When it comes to debt management, investing, or budgeting, people who have clear goals are better able to make decisions that support their overall financial vision.

7. **Bringing Actions and Aspirations Together:**Establishing definite financial targets guarantees that deeds correspond with ambitions. Readers are asked to describe their ideal lifestyle and the financial turning points that will get them there. A sense of congruence between current behaviors and future aspirations is fostered by this alignment.

8. **Increasing Resilience in the Face of Difficulties:** Achieving financial success is not without its difficulties. Well-defined financial objectives serve as pillars in trying times, giving people resilience and a feeling of purpose. Resilience is essential for overcoming obstacles and maintaining the millionaire mindset.

"Think and Act Like a Millionaire" essentially emphasizes how important it is to have specific financial goals as a habit that can change lives. Beyond only financial planning, it instills a mindset that prioritizes achievement, purpose, and deliberate actions—all crucial components for anyone hoping to achieve long-term financial success.

Creating a Strategic Financial Plan

In the framework of "Think and Act Like a Millionaire: The Essentials Strategies for Financial Success," one of the most important steps toward developing the coveted millionaire mindset is the formulation of a strategic financial plan. This is an examination of the reasons that, in the context of the book, this practice is considered essential:

Vision into Action: Turning the goal of financial success into doable actions is accomplished through the development of a strategic financial plan. The book helps readers express their goals before methodically outlining the specific actions required to make those goals a reality.

Goal Alignment: By serving as a compass, the strategic financial plan makes sure that the steps performed to attain financial goals are in line with each other. It offers a path that pushes people in the direction of their specified goals, encouraging a sense of purpose and direction in their financial journey

Resource Allocation and Prioritization: Careful resource allocation and financial activity prioritization are essential components of a strategic financial plan. It is recommended that readers determine which aspects of their financial lives have the greatest influence and allocate resources, such as income, savings, or investments, to the areas that have the greatest impact on their financial performance.

Strategies for Risk Management: The book acknowledges the significance of foreseeing and controlling financial hazards. A strategic financial strategy helps people protect their wealth against unanticipated obstacles and minimize future setbacks by implementing risk management techniques.

Budgeting for Success: The strategic financial plan's foundation is budgeting. The book helps readers create realistic budgets that are in line with their financial objectives. Readers can make sure that their financial resources are used effectively to maximize wealth-building potential by carefully planning and regulating spending.

Flexibility in Response to Changing Conditions: The strategic financial strategy is flexible. The text admits that economic conditions and human circumstances change throughout time. In order to stay flexible and steadfast in their pursuit of their millionaire mentality objectives, readers are urged to periodically assess and modify their plans.

investing and Wealth-Building Techniques: "Think and Act Like a Millionaire" offers guidance on successful wealth-building and investing techniques. A well-crafted financial plan helps people choose investments that match their risk appetite and long-term goals, which helps them accumulate wealth over time.

Continuous Assessment and Improvement: The significance of ongoing assessment and improvement is emphasized throughout the book. A strategic financial plan is a dynamic process that needs to be reviewed on a regular basis; it is not a one-time project. By using an iterative process, people can make necessary adjustments and are guaranteed to be on pace to accomplish their financial goals.

Encouraging Proactive Decision-Making: Making proactive decisions is encouraged when a strategic financial strategy is created. It empowers people to take charge of their financial future, make deliberate decisions, and actively direct their financial course toward their goals—a mindset necessary to become a millionaire.

To put it another way, in the context of "Think and Act Like a Millionaire: The Essentials Strategies for Financial Success," developing a strategic financial plan is a journey rather than just a useful task. It gives people the confidence to take control of their financial destiny, match their goals with their actions, and develop the kind of thinking that leads to long-term success and wealth building.

CHAPTER 3: WEALTH BUILDING STRATEGIES

Wealth Building Strategies:

DEFINITION

Wealth Building Strategies are deliberate, methodical methods and practices people use to gradually increase and broaden their financial holdings. In order to raise net worth and foster long-term success, these tactics entail more than just generating income; they also entail careful planning, responsible financial practices, and wise investment choices. Building wealth involves a number of activities, such as investing, managing debt, saving, and general financial planning, all aimed at reaching financial independence and ensuring a pleasant future. Smart financial choices, risk management, and a dedication to long-term financial objectives are frequently combined in successful wealth development techniques.

I've come to the conclusion that accumulating Wealth and being Wealthy aren't that difficult. It really is that easy.
It's certainly not simple. Many will never make it "rich," no matter how hard they work all their lives.
However, you are likely to Acquire enormous Wealth if you adhere to the fundamentals, which are the same core financial principles that have been employed by almost every extremely wealthy people throughout history.

1. Anyone can achieve extreme wealth since having wealth is a mindset that says, "Think And Act Like A Millionaire." In some years back one of my uncle's (Mr Rogers Johnson) was previously penniless, much like a lot of people who are now quite wealthy. Furthermore, he owned more than a hundred of thousands of Dollar After his bakery business collapsed.

In Addition his failed bakery business has Left him with hundred thousand of dollars debt , Still, he declared himself to be a wealthy Man. With bewildering certainty, he told his wife and family, "I am a rich man!"
He was aware that he could raise his hands and give up on ever accumulating fortune. However, he didn't.
"He always Think And Act Like A Millionaire —
Even with the enormous "zero" in his bank account, he continued to believe in wealth more than ever. Subsequently, he has amassed hundreds of millions of dollars via his "Wealth Building Strategies.

2. It is rare to build enormous fortune unless you have a strong belief that you can.

This is the whole idea behind this books"Think And Act Like A Millionaire The path to Millionaire Mindset" and The first step in creating enormous Wealth is to have the mindset that you can achieve it; if you don't think you can, you most likely won't.
Naturally, thinking that you will be wealthy won't make it happen. But without thinking you can, it's almost impossible to accumulate enormous fortune.

You will probably get what you think you deserve when accumulating wealth.
"Until someone feels they can obtain something, they are not prepared for it. Belief is the necessary mental condition, not only want or hope.
Good news! Anyone can develop an inner conviction that they will amass enormous Wealth. Growing up in physical poverty and with "scarcity" ideas may make it very difficult for certain people to develop this identity ("Think And Act Like A Millionaire").

However, acquiring an "abundance" mindset that is, believing that you will always succeed is almost always a necessary condition for accumulating enormous wealth.

The way the rich and the poor/middle class view wealth is one of the key distinctions between them. For the wealthy, enormous riches is unavoidable. They believe that success is certain.

The majority of individuals don't really think they'll ever amass enormous Wealth. That kind of attitude makes them unlikely to Succeed.

Your mentality is where enormous riches is first built. You have a much higher chance of succeeding than someone who doesn't genuinely believe you can get wealthy.

3. The conventional wisdom suggests that you'll never be wealthy.

You have to walk to a different drummer's beat. The same beat that the affluent listen to. Get off the dance floor right away if the beat seems reasonable!,I've read a lot, and this was one of the most paradigm-shifting things I've ever come across.

Ignore the advice of the majority.This is a result of the fact that most individuals are not well off. Most people have bad financial habits, and are deeply in debt, and are impoverished.The majority of people overspend, fail to save, make no investments, and don't become financially literate.

How could you possibly heed their advice?"One of the reasons that millionaires are economically successful is that they think differently." —Thomas Stanley.

Consider the most typical financial advise you have heard throughout the years. It most likely contains suggestions such as:

Don't spend all your money.

Get a well-paying job that suits you.

Increase portfolio diversification.

Practice thrift

Avoid taking large financial chances.

Your greatest asset is your house.

Each month, pay off your credit card.

However, the most important financial books in the world claim that most of this advice is false.It's traditional counsel that keeps people from achieving significant riches. Most of the time, the concepts are founded in fear and risk avoidance. They're not big enough. Rich people don't deal with these issues.The tendency to defy the grain of accepted financial wisdom is one of the most prevalent traits of extremely wealthy people.

To put it Simply,For thousands of years, there has been a single process for accumulating enormous Wealth.

Being wealthy is a mindset. Don't take conventional advise; it's typically not beneficial. Make your finances function for you. If it becomes monotonous, don't give up. Don't stop investing in your education; work toward owning it.

Adhering to these principles alone won't bring prosperity. However, almost all significant finance methods exposed similar ideas.
You would be smart to practice them attentively if you wish to be become enormous Wealthy..

Investing Wisely

Investing Wisely: The Core Tenet of Millionaire Mindset

In the pursuit of a millionaire mindset outlined in "Think and Act Like a Millionaire: The Path to Millionaire Mindset," investing wisely emerges as a fundamental principle. Beyond mere financial transactions, this concept embodies a strategic and informed approach to deploying financial resources for long-term wealth growth.

Strategic Decision-Making: Investing wisely involves strategic decision-making that aligns with long-term financial goals. It transcends impulsive actions and embraces a deliberate approach, recognizing that each investment should contribute meaningfully to the overall wealth-building strategy.

Risk Management: A millionaire mindset acknowledges that all investments carry some level of risk. Investing wisely includes a thoughtful assessment of risk and the implementation of strategies to manage and mitigate potential downsides. It's about striking a balance between potential returns and the level of acceptable risk.

Diversification: The wisdom of diversification is a key aspect. Rather than putting all eggs in one basket, a millionaire mindset encourages spreading investments across various asset classes. This not only helps manage risk but also positions the investor to benefit from different market conditions.

Knowledge and Education: Investing wisely requires ongoing knowledge and education. The millionaire mindset involves staying informed about market trends, financial instruments, and economic factors. Continuous learning empowers individuals to make informed decisions and adapt their investment strategies to changing circumstances.

Long-Term Perspective: A cornerstone of investing wisely is adopting a long-term perspective. Millionaire-minded investors understand the value of patience and the compounding effect of time on their investments. This perspective allows them to weather short-term market fluctuations and focus on the bigger picture.

Alignment with Financial Goals: Every investment should align with overarching financial goals. Whether it's funding retirement, purchasing real estate, or achieving other milestones, the millionaire mindset ensures that each investment serves a specific purpose within the broader financial plan.

Active Management: Investing wisely involves active management rather than a passive approach. This doesn't necessarily mean constant trading but rather periodic reviews, adjustments, and a proactive stance to capitalize on emerging opportunities or navigate changing market conditions.

Emotional Discipline: Maintaining emotional discipline is paramount. The millionaire mindset steers clear of emotional decision-making, recognizing that fear and greed can lead to impulsive actions. Wisely investing requires a rational and disciplined approach, even during times of market volatility.

Socially Responsible Investing: A holistic approach to investing wisely may include considerations beyond financial returns. Socially responsible investing, where individuals align their investments with ethical, environmental, or social values, reflects a conscientious aspect of the millionaire mindset.

To Put It Simply, investing wisely, as advocated in "Think and Act Like a Millionaire: The Path to Millionaire Mindset," transcends the traditional notion of financial transactions. It embodies a mindset that values strategic decision-making, risk management, continuous learning, and a disciplined approach—all essential elements in the journey toward long-term wealth building and financial success.

Generating Multiple Streams of Income

Within the pages of "Think and Act Like a Millionaire: The Path to Millionaire Mindset," the idea of creating several revenue streams comes to light as a potent and revolutionary idea. As a crucial tactic for achieving financial success, the billionaire mindset promotes revenue stream diversification and strategic expansion in addition to the conventional dependence on a single source of income.

Diversification Beyond Employment: The traditional reliance on employment income alone is questioned by the millionaire mindset. It encourages people to look into different ways to make money, understanding that relying only on a paycheck could impede one's ability to grow and become resilient financially.

Entrepreneurial Ventures: Embracing an entrepreneurial spirit is a hallmark of the millionaire mindset. This involves identifying business opportunities, creating products or services, and establishing ventures that contribute additional streams of income. Entrepreneurship allows individuals to leverage their skills and passions to build wealth.

Investment Income: The millionaire mindset acknowledges the power of money working for you. Beyond regular employment, generating income from investments—such as dividends, interest, or capital gains—becomes a fundamental strategy. This includes investments in stocks, bonds, real estate, or other wealth-building vehicles.

Passive Income Streams: Passive income, where earnings are not directly tied to active involvement, is a cornerstone of the millionaire mindset. This may include rental income, royalties, dividends, or income generated from automated business processes. Passive income liberates individuals from the constraints of trading time for money.

Real Estate Ventures: Investing in real estate is often promoted as a key avenue for income diversification. Whether through rental properties, real estate development, or real estate investment trusts (REITs), real estate can provide both ongoing income and long-term appreciation.

Side Businesses and Freelancing: The millionaire mindset recognizes the potential of side businesses and freelancing activities. Supplementing a primary income with earnings from freelance work or a side business not only boosts financial inflows but also hones entrepreneurial skills.

Digital Income Streams: In the modern era, the millionaire mindset explores digital income opportunities. This includes online businesses, affiliate marketing, e-commerce ventures, and creating digital products. The digital landscape offers diverse avenues for income generation with a global reach.

Continuous Learning and Skill Monetization: The journey to multiple income streams is intertwined with continuous learning. The millionaire mindset values acquiring new skills and finding ways to monetize them. This could involve offering training courses, consulting services, or creating products based on acquired expertise.

Strategic Partnerships and Collaborations: Collaborations and partnerships amplify the millionaire mindset's effectiveness. By leveraging networks and forming strategic alliances, individuals can create synergies that lead to new income opportunities and mutually beneficial ventures.

In summary, generating multiple streams of income, as advocated in "Think and Act Like a Millionaire: The Path to Millionaire Mindset," is a paradigm shift. It is a mindset that transcends the limitations of relying on a single source of income, embracing diversity, innovation, and strategic thinking to create a robust and resilient financial foundation.

CHAPTER 4: SMART MONEY HABITS

SMART Money Habits: A Blueprint for Millionaire Mindset

In the context of "Think and Act Like a Millionaire: The Path to Millionaire Mindset," adopting SMART money habits becomes a transformative approach to financial success. SMART, an acronym representing Specific, Measurable, Achievable, Relevant, and Time-bound, outlines a framework for cultivating disciplined and purposeful financial practices. Here's an exploration of SMART money habits, accompanied by examples within the millionaire mindset philosophy:

Specific:
Example: Instead of a vague goal like "saving money," a specific goal within the millionaire mindset could be "saving $10,000 over the next 12 months for an emergency fund."

Measurable:
Example: Rather than a general intention to "reduce debt," a measurable goal might be "paying off $5,000 of credit card debt within the next six months."

Achievable:
Example: Instead of setting an unrealistic target like "investing $50,000 in stocks tomorrow," an achievable goal could be "consistently investing 10% of monthly income in a diversified portfolio."

Relevant:
Example: Instead of pursuing a goal that doesn't align with overall financial objectives, a relevant goal might be "increasing contributions to retirement accounts to ensure financial security in retirement."

Time-bound:
Example: Rather than an open-ended commitment like "start a side business someday," a time-bound goal could be "launching a freelance consultancy within the next three months and earning $1,000 per month by the end of the year."

Explanation of SMART Money Habits:

❖ Budgeting with Precision:SMART money habits involve creating a detailed budget with specific allocations for expenses, savings, and investments. Measurable goals within the budget ensure adherence and progress tracking, such as setting aside a specific amount for monthly savings or debt repayment.

❖ Setting Measurable Savings Targets:The millionaire mindset emphasizes measurable savings targets, like saving a specific amount each month. Achievable goals ensure that the savings target is realistic and manageable, allowing for consistent progress toward financial goals.

❖ Investing Strategically:SMART investing involves setting specific investment goals, whether it's a target percentage return or a predefined portfolio diversification. Relevant investment choices align with overall financial objectives, and time-bound strategies guide decision-making and periodic reviews.

❖ Debt Reduction with Clear Targets:The millionaire mindset adopts SMART approaches to debt reduction, specifying clear targets for paying down debts. This involves setting achievable and relevant goals, such as paying off high-interest debts first within a designated timeframe.

❖ Creating Emergency Funds with Purpose:Establishing an emergency fund is a specific and achievable SMART money habit. Relevant to financial stability, this involves setting a measurable target, like saving three to six months' worth of living expenses, within a defined time frame.

❖ Continual Learning for Financial Literacy:SMART money habits extend to continual learning about personal finance. Specific goals could include reading a certain number of financial books or attending relevant workshops, ensuring ongoing improvement in financial literacy.

❖ Negotiating and Increasing Income Strategically:Within the millionaire mindset, SMART money habits encompass specific and measurable goals for negotiating salary raises or diversifying income streams. Achievable steps could include acquiring new skills to enhance marketability, setting specific income targets, and working towards them within a set timeframe.

- ❖ Regular Review and Adjustment:Time-bound SMART money habits involve regular reviews of financial goals and adjusting strategies as needed. This ensures that financial plans remain relevant, achievable, and aligned with the ever-evolving millionaire mindset.

In conclusion, adopting SMART money habit is a transformative approach. It's about infusing purpose, discipline, and strategic thinking into financial practices, ultimately paving the way for lasting financial success and the cultivation of a millionaire mindset.

Budgeting for Success

Elon Musk's Success Story: Using Budgeting to Your Advantage for Exceptional Results
The man behind Tesla and SpaceX, Elon Musk, is a visionary entrepreneur who personifies the ideas presented in "Think and Act Like a Millionaire: The Path to Millionaire Mindset."

Musk's success story demonstrates not just his inventiveness and audacious endeavors but also his savvy financial management, which includes efficient budgeting. Let's examine how Musk's strategy fits with the theory of the millionaire mindset:

Establishing Explicit Financial Goals: Elon Musk's journey commenced with unambiguous financial objectives. He began his profession with the goal of revolutionizing space travel and transportation. From Zip2 to PayPal, SpaceX, and Tesla, each endeavor was a step closer to reaching these audacious financial goals.

Measurable Objectives in Ambitious Ventures: Every endeavor in Musk's success story has quantifiable objectives. Whether it was hitting electric vehicle production milestones at Tesla or landing lucrative contracts and launches at SpaceX, Musk made sure his objectives were clear, measurable, and consistent with his overall vision.

Achievable Innovation Steps: Musk's success with budgeting is linked to the innovative actions he took that were attainable. Even with lofty objectives, Musk took a step at a time to tackle each problem. By using a methodical approach, he was able to overcome challenges and work around financial limits, which set him up for long-term success.

Appropriate deployment of Resources: Musk's success story demonstrates appropriate and deliberate resource deployment. The essential requirements of each enterprise, such as investing in state-of-the-art technology for SpaceX or streamlining production procedures at Tesla, were the focal point of budgetary decisions. Resources were always allocated by Musk where they would have the biggest effects on his objectives.

Flexibility and Ongoing Education: Musk exemplifies the principles of the millionaire mindset, which include flexibility and ongoing education. His accomplishments are characterized by his readiness to review spending plans, change course when required, and keep ahead of market developments. This flexibility guarantees that financial plans stay applicable when faced with changing obstacles.

Musk's business endeavors are inherently risky, but his track record of success demonstrates a calculated approach to risk and return management. The calculated risks connected with each project were taken into consideration while creating the budget, ensuring that funds were used wisely to optimize the likelihood of success.

Temporary Innovation: The success of Elon Musk serves as a reminder of the value of growth and innovation that is time-bound. The urgency and time sensitivity inherent in the fast expanding businesses he entered informed his budgeting decisions, whether it was completing launch dates at SpaceX or reaching profitability at Tesla within a set timeline.

In conclusion, Elon Musk's success story serves as evidence of the millionaire mindset, which views budgeting as a strategic compass that steers bold endeavors and aspirational goals in addition to a financial tool. Musk is a perfect example of the transformational potential of thinking and acting like a millionaire because of his ability to combine vision with sensible money management.

Effective Saving Techniques

Within the context of "Essentials Strategies for Financial Success," effective saving techniques serve as the bedrock for building financial stability and achieving long-term goals. Let's explore and explain key strategies that contribute to successful saving:

Automated Savings:
- Explanation: Set up automatic transfers to a dedicated savings account. This technique ensures consistency and discipline in saving by treating it as a non-negotiable monthly expense.

Pay Yourself First:
- Explanation: Prioritize savings by allocating a portion of your income before addressing other expenses. Treat savings as a non-negotiable part of your budget, reinforcing the habit of paying yourself first.

Create a Budget:
- Explanation: Develop a detailed budget that outlines income, expenses, and savings goals. A budget provides a clear roadmap for managing money, identifying areas for potential savings, and avoiding unnecessary expenditures.

Set Specific Savings Goals:
- Explanation: Define clear and specific savings goals, such as an emergency fund, a vacation fund, or a down payment for a home. Having tangible objectives provides motivation and direction for your saving efforts.

Track and Trim Expenses:
- Explanation: Regularly track expenses to identify areas where you can cut back. Eliminating unnecessary spending allows you to redirect funds towards savings, accelerating your progress toward financial goals.

Emergency Fund Prioritization:
- Explanation: Prioritize building an emergency fund. This fund acts as a financial safety net, providing peace of mind and preventing the need to dip into long-term savings for unexpected expenses.

Take Advantage of Employer Benefits:
- Explanation: Maximize employer benefits, such as retirement contributions or matching programs. This ensures that you're leveraging additional sources of income to bolster your savings.

Consolidate and Negotiate Debts:
- Explanation: If you have multiple debts, consider consolidating them for easier management. Additionally, negotiate interest rates to reduce the overall cost of debt, freeing up more funds for savings.

Review Adjust Regularly:
- Explanation: Regularly review your financial situation and adjust your savings strategy as needed. Life circumstances change, and your savings plan should adapt to reflect new goals or challenges.

Explore High-Interest Savings Accounts:
- Explanation: Look for savings accounts with competitive interest rates. High-interest accounts help your savings grow faster, maximizing the returns on your efforts.

Cash Windfalls for Savings:
- Explanation: Allocate unexpected windfalls, such as tax refunds or bonuses, directly to savings. This accelerates progress toward your goals without impacting your regular budget.

Practice Frugality Mindfully:
- Explanation: Embrace frugality consciously by making mindful spending choices. Differentiate between needs and wants, allocating more resources to essentials and saving the surplus.

Utilize Technology for Savings:
- Explanation: Leverage budgeting apps, automatic transfers, and financial tools to streamline and optimize your savings process. Technology can help you stay organized and committed to your goals.

Educate Yourself on Personal Finance:
- Explanation: Invest time in educating yourself on personal finance. Understanding financial principles empowers you to make informed decisions and develop effective saving strategies tailored to your unique situation.

Incorporating these effective saving techniques into your financial toolkit, as outlined in "Essentials Strategies for Financial Success," positions you on the path to building a solid financial foundation and achieving your long-term objectives. Remember, successful saving is not just about the amount saved but the deliberate and consistent effort put into the process.

Myths and Realities

"Think and Act Like a Millionaire" debunks popular misconceptions about accumulating wealth and replaces them with sobering facts that are consistent with the millionaire mindset. This essay examines a few common myths and the associated realities:

Myth:
Only High-Paying Jobs Can Bring Wealth
Reality: Although having a large salary is advantageous, actual riches frequently comes from careful money management, astute investment, and several sources of income. The millionaire mindset acknowledges that there are other ways to create wealth besides a wage, such as through investments and entrepreneurship.

Myth
 High Risks Are Always Taken by Millionaires
Reality: Rather of taking chances blindly, those with a millionaire mindset take measured risks. A balanced approach to risk management, extensive study, and well-informed decision-making are frequently prerequisites for successful wealth building. Risk-taking in a prudent manner supports long-term financial objectives.

Myth:
 The Lifestyles of Millionaires Are Luxurious
The truth is that not all wealthy lead ostentatious lives. Many become thrifty, put money security first, and concentrate on accumulating riches rather than flaunting it. The millionaire mindset places a strong emphasis on prudent spending, calculated risks, and living below one's means.

Myth:

Getting Rich Is Something That Happens Overnight Developing significant wealth is a slow process that calls on effort and discipline. The significance of consistency, long-term planning, and gradually modifying tactics is acknowledged by the millionaire mindset. Success that comes easily to you after years of hard work usually last.

Myth:
The Main Source of Wealth Is Inheritance Reality: Although some billionaires come from wealthy families, many self-made millionaires build their fortunes via perseverance, resourcefulness, and astute financial planning. The mindset of a millionaire places a high importance on independence and constantly searches out chances to advance financially.

Myth:
Having money makes you happy
As it is The millionaire mindset understands that although having money is important, it doesn't ensure happiness on its own. A successful and happy life requires emotional health, meaningful relationships, and personal development.

Myth:
Freedom Is Limited by Budgeting
The truth is that, far from limiting financial independence, budgeting is a tool that enhances it. Budgeting, according to the millionaire mindset, offers a path for deliberate spending, saving, and investing that promotes flexibility and control over one's financial future.

Myth:
Only Experts Should Pursue Financial Education
Reality: Everyone is encouraged to continue their financial education by adopting a billionaire attitude. Gaining a fundamental understanding of finance is crucial for managing money wisely, making well-informed decisions, and laying the groundwork for long-term financial success.

Myth:
 Having Wealth Depends on Chance or Luck
Reality: Although outside circumstances do matter, the millionaire mindset places a strong emphasis on taking charge of one's own life and making proactive decisions. While occasionally luck may play a role, consistent riches is typically the outcome of intentional acts, perseverance, and a success-oriented mindset.

To sum up, "Think and Act Like a Millionaire" dispels myths on how to build wealth and fosters an attitude based on doable tactics, self-control, and a comprehensive approach to achievement. People who are aware of the truths underlying these beliefs can successfully travel the path to

CHAPTER 5: ENTREPRENEURIAL MINDSET

An entrepreneurial mindset is a particular way of thinking and tackling problems that is frequently connected to business owners. It encompasses a range of traits, mindsets, and actions that enable people to spot opportunities, take calculated chances, and come up with creative solutions. An entrepreneurial mindset is characterized by several essential components, such as a readiness to accept uncertainty, a proactive approach to problem-solving, flexibility in the face of change, a commitment to lifelong learning, perseverance in the face of failure, and an acute awareness of and ability to seize growth and success-oriented opportunities. This type of entrepreneur frequently demonstrates inventiveness, ingenuity, and a strong desire to turn concepts into successful businesses or breakthroughs.

In the ever-changing world of business, the entrepreneurial mindset serves as a beacon that points people in the direction of opportunity, creativity, and success.

The fundamental quality of an entrepreneurial mindset is a strong willingness to accept ambiguity. This kind of attitude sees hurdles as opportunities for innovation rather than barriers facing entrepreneurs. They flourish in dynamic settings where they may use change as an opportunity for advancement rather than as a hindrance.

An essential component of the entrepreneurial mindset is proactivity. People with this mentality are issue solvers and initiators rather than just being observers. To transform prospects into businesses, they look for openings, spot market gaps, and take measured risks.

Another important component is adaptability. The necessity to adapt when circumstances change and the dynamic nature of corporate environments are both acknowledged by the entrepreneurial mindset. Those that have this perspective accept change as an essential component of the entrepreneurial path, as opposed to fighting it.

The entrepreneurial attitude is threaded throughout with a constant state of learning. Entrepreneurs are aware that continuing education is essential to remaining inventive and current. They look for fresh information, absorb lessons from past mistakes, and use newfound understanding to hone their tactics.

One essential component of the entrepreneurial mindset is resilience. Being an entrepreneur is a journey filled with ups and downs, therefore it's critical to have the resilience to overcome obstacles. This kind of entrepreneur sees setbacks as teaching moments and turns them into lessons learned for next time.

Seeing and seizing chances is a distinguishing quality. An acute sense of observation allows entrepreneurs with an entrepreneurial mindset to spot market gaps and come up with original solutions. Where others would perceive obstacles, they perceive opportunities.

The entrepreneurial attitude unleashes creativity and resourcefulness. Entrepreneurs are great problem solvers who frequently make the most impact with little in the way of resources. One of the motivators is the capacity for unconventional thought.

The entrepreneurial mindset is, at its core, a dynamic force that inspires people to take transformative action. Adopting this attitude enables people to actively create and redefine the business environment in addition to navigating its intricacies, whether they are starting a company, leading a team inside an enterprise, or pursuing personal endeavors. As we go into this examination of the entrepreneurial mindset, we expose the fundamental ideas behind it, its influence on a range of disciplines, and doable tactics for developing and utilizing it in a variety of contexts.

TYPES OF ENTREPRENEURIAL MINDSET

There are several forms of the entrepreneurial mindset, and they are all distinguished by unique attitudes, strategies, and priorities. The following are a few varieties of entrepreneurial mindsets:

1. **Innovative Mindset:** This mindset places a strong emphasis on innovation. Innovative entrepreneurs are always looking for new methods to enhance their goods, procedures, or services. They are passionate about pushing boundaries, embracing originality, and question the current quo.

2. **Growth mentality**: The conviction that learning and progress are lifelong pursuits is what defines a growth mentality. This kind of mentality allows entrepreneurs to view obstacles as chances to improve their abilities. They are receptive to criticism, grow from mistakes, and persevere in the face of difficulties.

3. **Social Entrepreneurial Mindset**: Along with achieving financial success, social entrepreneurs prioritize making a positive social impact. They see business as a tool to further the common good and are motivated by a desire to find solutions to social or environmental problems.

4. **Tech-Savvy attitude**: In the quickly changing world of technology, entrepreneurs that possess this attitude are skilled at using technology to spur innovation. They use digital tools, keep up with new developments in technology, and look to technology to solve problems in the business world.

5. **mindset of a serial entrepreneur:**The mindset of a serial entrepreneur is that of someone who regularly launches and expands new businesses. Their attitude is defined by their propensity for seeing new chances, comfort with risk, and expertise juggling the demands of several projects.

6. **Corporate Entrepreneurial Mindset:**Within established organizations, individuals with a corporate entrepreneurial mindset, also known as "intrapreneurs," exhibit entrepreneurial traits. They drive innovation within the corporate structure, introducing new ideas, products, or processes to spur growth and competitiveness.

7. **Lean Startup Mindset**: This type of entrepreneurship places a strong emphasis on resource optimization and efficiency. To achieve product-market fit in an economical way, they put a lot of emphasis on rapidly testing concepts, iterating in response to feedback, and cutting back on needless expenses.

8. **consumer-Centric Mindset**: This way of thinking emphasizes the importance of comprehending and satisfying consumer needs. Customer-centric entrepreneurs place a high importance on establishing rapport, providing value, and modifying their products in response to input from clients.

9. **Disruptive Mindset**: Disruptive entrepreneurs question accepted conventions and sectors of the economy. They use cutting-edge concepts and innovations to aim to transform established markets. Having a disruptive mindset is being prepared to question status quo and present novel ideas.

10. **Global perspective**: Businesspeople that have a global perspective see beyond national boundaries. They are aware of global trends, various cultural contexts, and foreign markets. This way of thinking entails being open to growing businesses abroad and modifying plans to fit various market conditions.

These entrepreneurial mindsets don't have to conflict with one another; depending on their experiences, objectives, and type of business, entrepreneurs may display a mix of these characteristics. People with an entrepreneurial mindset can succeed in a variety of entrepreneurial pursuits and adapt to a variety of conditions thanks to its versatility.

Identifying Opportunities

The key to success in the dynamic world of entrepreneurship is the capacity to recognize opportunities. An open mind, a keen sense of observation, and the willingness to turn obstacles into opportunities are prerequisites for embarking on an entrepreneurial adventure. This introduction delves into the essence of opportunity identification, a critical ability that drives people toward innovation, development, and the fulfillment of their entrepreneurial dreams.

The Secret to Seizing Opportunities: The essence of entrepreneurship is the ability to identify opportunities where others see obstacles. Finding chances requires more than just luck; it involves a purposeful, proactive approach that looks for possible channels for generating profit. The ability to identify gaps, inefficiencies, or unmet requirements in any area—business, technology, or social impact—fuels the entrepreneurial journey

The Entrepreneurial Lens: Those that are successful see the world differently, seeing challenges as chances for growth and impediments as doors to creativity. People might see opportunities that others might miss, question the status quo, and challenge conventional thinking by using this lens. Developing an entrepreneurial mindset in which every issue is a blank slate for original solutions is necessary for spotting chances.

Adaptability and Market Dynamics: In dynamic and constantly shifting market environments, the entrepreneurial journey takes place. Adaptability and a thorough comprehension of market dynamics are necessary for opportunity identification. In order to position themselves to take advantage of possibilities as they present themselves, entrepreneurs keep abreast of developing trends, technology developments, and changes in customer behavior.

Innovation as a Catalyst: The act of seeing opportunities is entwined with innovation. Entrepreneurs have an attitude that encourages original thought and looks for fresh solutions to problems that already exist. People can seize possibilities for ground-breaking innovations that set them apart in cutthroat markets by cultivating an innovative culture.

From Challenges to Solutions: Turning obstacles into solutions is a necessary step in spotting opportunities. Entrepreneurs use challenges as opportunities for innovation, posing queries such as "What unmet needs can we address?" and "How can this be done differently?" This change in viewpoint makes it possible to spot opportunities that result in significant and effective solutions.

Risk-Taking and Strategic Exploration: Entrepreneurs are risk-takers who strategically explore new ground in pursuit of possibilities. To do this, one must be prepared to venture beyond of one's comfort zone, accept ambiguity, and take measured risks. Finding chances frequently entails taking calculated risks in the unknown, where doing so can lead to success.

Finding possibilities gives entrepreneurial dreamers the ability to influence the future and foster their business vision. It entails imagining a scenario in which demands are anticipated before they become evident and solutions are not only reactive but proactive. By having this vision, business owners present themselves as the creators of advancement and constructive change.

Building a Successful Business

Setting out to create a profitable business is a dynamic and life-changing adventure. It takes a combination of fortitude, strategic thinking, vision, and a thorough comprehension of the complex dance between creativity and execution. This introduction lays the groundwork for discussing important ideas, useful tactics, and the entrepreneurial spirit necessary to build a successful and long-lasting company enterprise.

The Key to Creating a Successful Business: Creating a successful business involves more than just developing a good or service; it also entails creating an organization that can change, grow, and leave a lasting impression in addition to satisfying consumer needs. At its foundation, the desire to solve issues, satisfy unmet needs, and make a significant contribution to society is what drives entrepreneurs in their quest to establish profitable businesses.

Visionary Leadership: At the core of any flourishing company is visionary leadership. Entrepreneurs that set out on this path do so with a compelling vision that goes beyond short-term objectives. This vision serves as a beacon of light, directing the company through difficulties, motivating groups, and coordinating all efforts toward a common goal.

Innovation and Adaptability: These two qualities are the twin engines of success in the quick-changing and highly innovative world of business. Developing a profitable company requires ongoing innovation in all areas, including procedures, goods, and customer experiences.
The ability to adapt guarantees that the company will withstand changes in the market and advances in technology.

client-Centric Approach: A thorough grasp of the client is the foundation of any successful business. Developing a customer-centric business is more than just offering goods or services; it also entails addressing problems, fostering connections, and continuously giving value. When a company becomes a vital part of its clients' lives, it succeeds.

Strategic preparation and Execution: Careful execution combined with strategic preparation paves the way for success. Entrepreneurs have a complex dance to learn: how to set realistic objectives, create winning strategies, and carry out plans precisely. Achieving this approach requires striking a balance between agility, foresight, and a steadfast dedication to performance.

Resilience in the Face of Difficulties: Being an entrepreneur is a difficult road that is full of unknowns, disappointments, and unanticipated hurdles. Resilience is the quality needed to weather storms, learn from mistakes, and come out stronger in order to build a successful business. Challenges become chances for improvement and development when one is resilient.

Team Building and Culture: The combined efforts of a committed team are what make every firm strong; no one company can succeed on its own. Entrepreneurs need to put a lot of effort into developing a culture of teamwork and positivity where all employees share the same vision for the business. A well-functioning team enhances creativity, output, and general success.

Ethical and Sustainable behaviors: Ethical and sustainable behaviors lay the road to success. Companies that put integrity, social responsibility, and environmental sustainability first not only make a great impact on the world, but also cultivate long-lasting relationships with stakeholders and clients.

We peel back the layers of creative thinking, strategic thinking, and the complex nature of entrepreneurship as we set out to explore creating a profitable company. With the help of practical examples, insights that can be put into practice, and a thorough knowledge of the entrepreneurial ecosystem, we help those who want to transform their idea into a successful and meaningful business enterprise.

Rich entrepreneurs' strategic and visionary efforts frequently pave the path from vision to a thriving and successful business. These people build organizations that endure throughout time by utilizing their resources, expertise, and insights in addition to amassing cash. Here, we explore prominent business-building techniques used by affluent businesspeople.

1. Visionary Investment in Innovation: Wealthy entrepreneurs recognize the transformative power of innovation. They invest strategically in groundbreaking ideas, cutting-edge technologies, and disruptive solutions that have the potential to revolutionize industries. By staying at the forefront of innovation, they position their businesses as leaders in a rapidly evolving market.

2. Diversification and Risk Management: Successful businesses crafted by wealthy entrepreneurs often reflect a diversified portfolio. By spreading investments across different industries or asset classes, they mitigate risks associated with economic fluctuations. Diversification enables them to navigate uncertainties and capitalize on opportunities in varied sectors.

3. Long-Term Strategic Planning: Wealthy entrepreneurs adopt a long-term perspective in building their businesses. Their strategic planning extends beyond immediate gains, focusing on

sustainable growth and enduring value. This foresight allows them to make decisions that contribute to the longevity and resilience of their enterprises.

4. Leveraging Networks and Relationships: Networking is a cornerstone for wealthy entrepreneurs in business building. They leverage extensive networks and cultivate meaningful relationships with industry leaders, influencers, and other entrepreneurs. These connections open doors to collaborations, partnerships, and valuable insights that contribute to business success.

5. Continuous Learning and Adaptability: The journey of building a successful business is marked by a commitment to continuous learning. Wealthy entrepreneurs remain curious, adapt to evolving market dynamics, and stay abreast of industry trends. This dedication to learning equips them with the knowledge needed to make informed decisions in a rapidly changing business landscape.

6. Strategic Use of Capital: Wealthy entrepreneurs understand the strategic use of capital. Whether through self-funding, venture capital, or strategic partnerships, they deploy financial resources judiciously. This involves making calculated investments in key areas such as research and development, marketing, and talent acquisition to drive sustainable growth.

7. Emphasis on Company Culture and Talent Acquisition: Successful businesses led by wealthy entrepreneurs prioritize company culture and talent acquisition. They build organizations with a shared vision, values, and a positive work environment. By attracting and retaining top-tier talent, these entrepreneurs create teams that are instrumental in executing strategic objectives and fostering innovation.

8. Social Responsibility and Ethical Practices: Wealthy entrepreneurs often integrate social responsibility and ethical practices into their business models. Recognizing the importance of corporate citizenship, they engage in philanthropy, sustainable practices, and initiatives that contribute positively to society. This approach not only enhances brand reputation but aligns the business with broader societal goals.

9. **Adaptation of Technology and Digital Transformation**: In the digital age, wealthy entrepreneurs recognize the imperative of technology adoption. They embrace digital

transformation to enhance efficiency, improve customer experiences, and stay competitive. The strategic integration of technology becomes a catalyst for growth and resilience in the evolving business landscape.

10. Resilience in the Face of Difficulties: Growing a profitable company is not without its difficulties. Rich businesspeople show resiliency in the face of difficulty. They see obstacles as teaching opportunities, change course when called upon, and stay steadfastly committed to their goal even in the face of adversity.

Essentially, affluent entrepreneurs use techniques other than financial competence to develop successful enterprises. They are visionaries who also possess strategic thinking, flexibility, and a dedication to moral and sustainable business methods. Through examining these strategies, would-be business owners can learn a great deal about the complex process of building long-lasting as well as significant companies.

Personal Stories or Example

Success Story:

The Resilient Entrepreneur

Introducing Sarah Rodriguez, a budding businesswoman whose journey demonstrates the strength of perseverance and enterprise. The beginning of Sarah's tale is marked by a setback: she lost her job amid a recession. Rather than giving in to hopelessness, Sarah used this as a chance to rethink her course.

Phase 1: Finding Possibilities in Difficulties
Sarah, unfazed by her jobless status, saw a need for individualized wellness programs. Inspired by her personal experiences with stress and mental health, she imagined a platform that provided customized programs for well-being. Her entrepreneurial journey began with this initial spark.

Phase 2: Strategic Planning and Visionary Innovation
Sarah innovated because she was devoted to her vision. She worked with IT specialists and medical professionals to create an intuitive app that offered individualized advice on mental health and wellness. Thorough market research and a firm grasp of her target audience were essential components of her strategic planning.

Phase 3: Making Use of Support Networks
Sarah made use of her professional contacts, mentorships, and support systems because she understood the value of networks. She sought advice from seasoned businesspeople, building connections that led to insights, mentoring, and even possible investors for her project.

Phase Four: Handling Difficulties with Resilience
There are always difficulties on the path of entrepreneurship. Sarah encountered difficulties, such as initial skepticism from potential customers and technological issues during the app's introduction. But her tenacity turned into a motivating factor. She improved her product in response to feedback, honed her marketing plan, and persevered in the face of challenges.

Phase 5: Achievement and Beneficial Effect
Testimonials regarding Sarah's app's beneficial effects on users' wellbeing began to stream in as it gained popularity. What began as an attempt to overcome personal hardship developed into a successful company. Not only did her business succeed financially, but it also enabled her to achieve her goal of providing mental health services to as many people as possible.

Important lessons learned:
The Catalyst in Adversity: Sarah's story demonstrates the transformational impact of seeing hardship as a source of opportunity for growth. Her job loss served as the catalyst for her decision to pursue an entrepreneurial endeavor with a purpose.

Innovation and Resilience: Sarah overcame obstacles thanks to her creative thinking and unflinching resilience. She accepted failures as teaching moments and modified her approach accordingly.

Networks and Mentorship: Sarah's career was greatly influenced by her networks and mentorship. Making and using relationships gave her the advice, support, and insightful information she needed to successfully navigate the world of entrepreneurship.

Positive Impact: In addition to being financially successful, Sarah's business improved other people's quality of life. Her dedication to solving a social issue showed how entrepreneurship has the power to bring about significant change.

The success story of Sarah Rodriguez is a motivational example of the life-changing potential that come with pursuing an entrepreneurial career. It emphasizes how crucial resilience, inventiveness, and a visionary attitude are to overcoming obstacles and launching worthwhile projects.

CONCLUSION

Through the journey described in "Think and Act Like a Millionaire: The Path to Millionaire Mindset - Essentials Strategies for Financial Success," we have looked at the useful tactics and transforming ideas that open doors to abundance in money. Let's condense our learnings into a final analysis:

1. Developing a Wealth-Oriented Mindset: Developing a mindset that supports wealth development is the first step in achieving financial success. This entails changing viewpoints, letting go of restrictive ideas, and embracing the fundamental values that millionaires uphold.

2. Seeing possibilities and Coming Up with New Ideas: The billionaire mindset is all about seeing possibilities where obstacles exist. Millionaire-thinking and -acting entrepreneurs use creativity, flexibility, and a deep understanding of market dynamics to turn challenges into opportunities.

3. Creating Measurable and Unambiguous Financial Goals: Creating quantifiable and unambiguous goals is essential to financial success. Establishing and prioritizing financial objectives gives direction and purpose, whether one chooses to create a strategic financial plan or adopt budgeting practices.

4. Strategic Investment and Risk Management: Millionaires understand the art of strategic investment. From diversifying portfolios to navigating risks, a calculated and informed approach to financial decisions is a hallmark of the millionaire mindset.

5. Ongoing Education and Flexibility: Achieving financial success is a continuous process. Adopting an attitude of constant learning and flexibility guarantees that people stay ahead of the curve, skillfully and presciently handling changes in the financial landscape.

6. Creating Several Revenue Streams: Millionaires frequently amass money by creating a number of revenue streams. Through a variety of means, including side businesses, investments, and strategic alliances, people can build a solid and long-lasting financial base.

7.Making Financial Education a Priority: Having a strong commitment to financial education is a crucial aspect of the millionaire mindset. Knowing the nuances of personal finance gives people the ability to negotiate challenging financial situations, manage resources sensibly, and make well-informed decisions.

8.Balancing Risk and Return: A careful balance between risk and return is a key component of successful financial strategy. A measured strategy is used by millionaires to make decisions that are in line with their long-term financial goals by weighing prospective risks and rewards.

9.Building a Positive Money attitude: The development of a positive money attitude is essential to the millionaire mindset. Through the acceptance of abundance, the practice of appreciation, and the deliberate development of wealth-related attitudes, people can cultivate a mindset that attracts prosperity.

10.Strategic Financial Planning: This is the equivalent of a success road map. Millionaires understand the need of making long-term plans, tying financial objectives to doable actions, and periodically reviewing tactics to guarantee ongoing success.

Ultimately, "Think and Act Like a Millionaire: The Path to Millionaire Mindset -is an invitation to a life-changing experience rather than just a manual. In addition to achieving financial success, people may develop a mindset that transcends financial prosperity by implementing the ideas and tactics discussed here—a mindset that values abundance, creativity, and living with a purpose. The road to a Millionaire mindset is a dynamic and empowering one that invites everyone to follow it to create a fulfilling and prosperous financial future.

"From Zero to 100K: Seven Proven Strategies to Amplify Your Earnings in 90 Days"

1. **Introduction**

- A brief introduction to the book and the promise it holds.

Welcome to "From Zero to 100K: Seven Proven Strategies to Amplify Your Earnings in 90 Days". This book is your comprehensive guide to financial success, promising a journey that can turn your financial dreams into reality. The goal is simple: to help you make 100K in three months. While the task may seem daunting, with the right mindset and tools, it is entirely achievable.

This book is not just about making money, it's about transforming your relationship with money and empowering you to take control of your financial future. It's about understanding that wealth isn't a luxury, but a tool that can be used to create a fulfilling and secure life.

As you turn the pages, you'll discover seven proven strategies that have helped countless individuals achieve financial success. Each chapter is packed with practical advice, insightful tips, and real-life examples. We will cover a broad spectrum of strategies including investment, entrepreneurship, negotiation skills, online businesses, and real estate.

Whether you're a novice who's just starting out or someone with some experience looking to boost your income, this book has something for everyone. Firmly rooted in reality, this book will provide you with actionable strategies rather than theoretical concepts.

Remember, the journey to 100K in 90 days begins with a single step. As you embark on this journey, hold on to the promise that each strategy, each chapter, and each page holds for you. It's time to turn the page and take that step. Welcome to a journey of transformation and financial freedom. Welcome to "From Zero to 100K".

- Establishing the need for financial freedom and the possibilities that come with it.

Financial freedom is more than just having money. It's the freedom to be who you really are and do what you really want in life. Many of us lose sight of this by feeling trapped in jobs we hate, bills that seem endless, and societal pressures to conform to a certain lifestyle. However, it doesn't have to be this way. Financial freedom is achievable and it opens up a world of possibilities.

Imagine a life where you are not bound by the constraints of a 9-to-5 job, where you have the freedom to choose how you spend your time, whether that's pursuing a passion project, spending more time with family, or traveling the world. Imagine a life where you don't worry about living paycheck to paycheck, where you can afford the best education for your children, or where you can comfortably retire without the fear of running out of money.

Financial freedom allows you to live life on your own terms. It's about taking control and making decisions for your life without the stress of financial repercussions. It's about being able to weather life's financial ups and downs because you have a strong foundation.

This is not a dream. It's a reality for those who understand the value of money, not just as a means to buy things, but as a tool for creating wealth and securing financial freedom. The strategies laid out in this book can guide you on this journey, teaching you how to amplify your earnings, save wisely, invest smartly, and build a robust financial future.

The possibilities that come with financial freedom are limitless. It's about creating a life filled with meaning and purpose, where you are not just surviving, but thriving. Start your journey to financial freedom today and unlock the countless possibilities that await.